# Contents

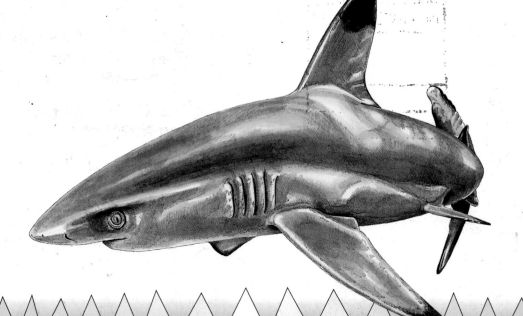

# What is a shark?

Sharks are cold-blooded sea creatures. They have muscular, streamlined bodies and breathe with gills. They are also very intelligent animals with large brains and good memories.

The biggest difference between sharks and fish is their skeleton. Fish have rigid skeletons made of bone, but sharks' skeletons are made of a flexible material called cartilage.

Fish have smooth skin covered in scales. Sharks have rough skin without scales. A fish's gills are covered and hard to see, but sharks' gills look like a line of slits with no covers.

Is a shark a fish?

No, a shark is not a fish!

Is a skate a fish?

No, a skate is not a fish!

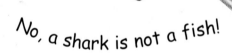

X-Ray Vision

Hold the page opposite up to the light and see what's inside a shark.

See what's inside

A skate has a cartilage skeleton, so it is related to sharks and is not a fish. Skate live on the seabed and hunt crabs, lobsters and octopuses.

4

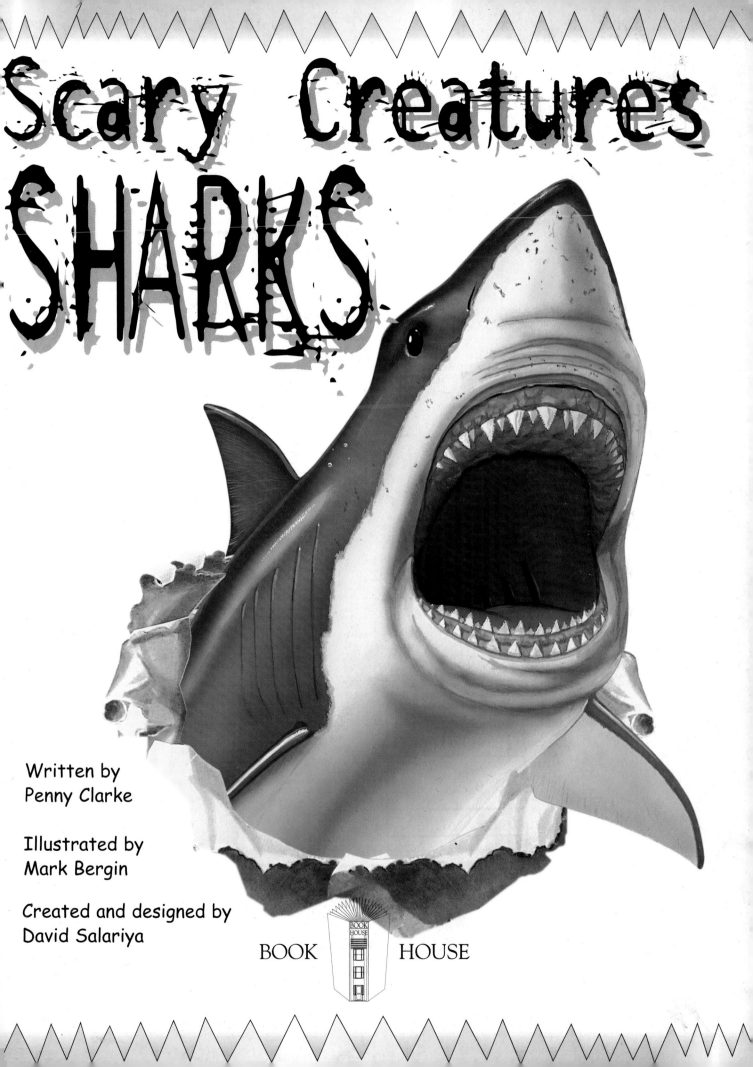

# Scary Creatures
# SHARKS

Written by
Penny Clarke

Illustrated by
Mark Bergin

Created and designed by
David Salariya

BOOK HOUSE

**Author:**

**Penny Clarke** is an author and editor specialising in information books for children. The books she has written include titles on natural history, rainforests and volcanoes, as well as others on different periods of history. She used to live in central London, but thanks to modern technology she has now realised her dream of being able to live and work in the countryside.

**Artist:**

**Mark Bergin** was born in Hastings in 1961. He studied at Eastbourne College of Art and has illustrated many children's non-fiction books. He lives in Bexhill-on-Sea with his wife and three children.

**Additional artists:**

Elizabeth Branch
Jackie Harland

**Series creator:**

**David Salariya** was born in Dundee, Scotland. In 1989 he established The Salariya Book Company. He has illustrated a wide range of books and has created many new series for publishers in the UK and overseas. He lives in Brighton with his wife, illustrator Shirley Willis, and their son.

**Consultant:**

**Dr Gerald Legg** holds a doctorate in zoology from Manchester University. He worked in West Africa for several years as a lecturer and rainforest researcher and his current position is biologist at the Booth Museum of Natural History in Brighton. He is also the author of many natural history books for children.

**Editors:**

Stephanie Cole
Karen Barker Smith

**Photographic credits:**

t=top, b=bottom

A.N.T, NHPA: 9, 18, 23, 29t
G I Bernard, NHPA: 27
Mark Bowler, NHPA: 22
Trevor McDonald, NHPA: 20
Merlin Entertaiments Group Ltd./Sea Life Centres: 29b
Linda & Brian Pitkin, NHPA: 8
Bill Wood, NHPA: 26
Norbert Wu, NHPA: 16, 17

Published in Great Britain in 2002 by
Book House, an imprint of
**The Salariya Book Company Ltd**
25 Marlborough Place, Brighton BN1 1UB

Visit the Salariya Book Company at
**www. salariya.com**
**www.book-house.co.uk**

A catalogue record for this book is available from the British Library.

ISBN  1 904194 23 0

Printed in Italy.

Printed on paper from sustainable forests.

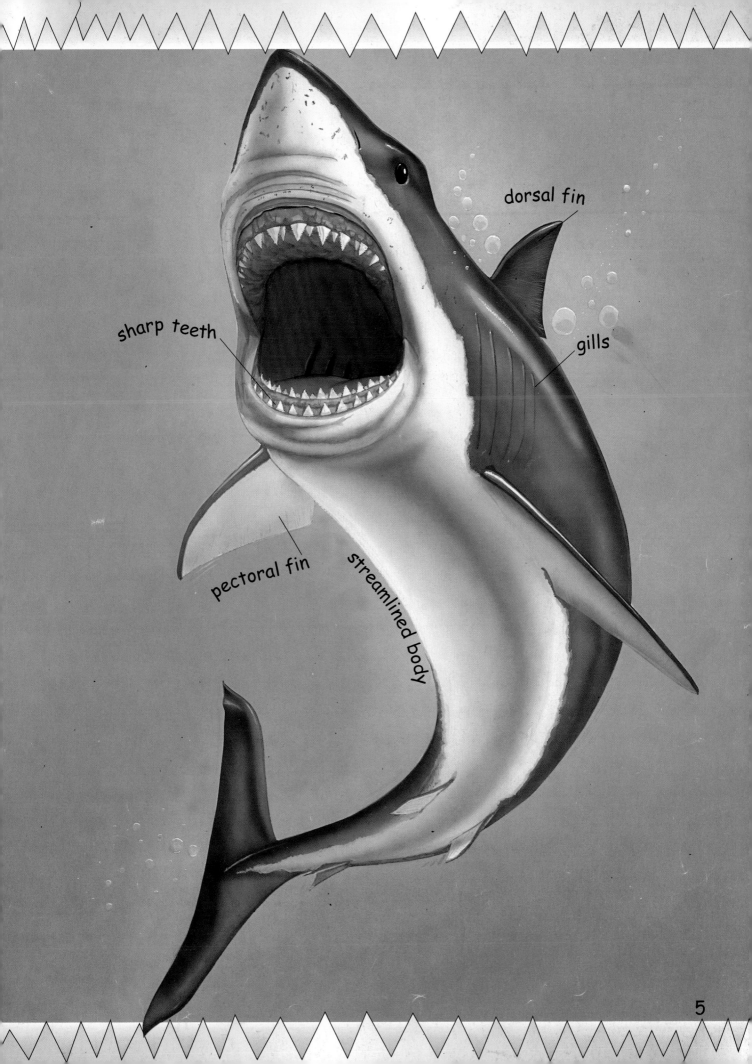

dorsal fin

sharp teeth

gills

pectoral fin

streamlined body

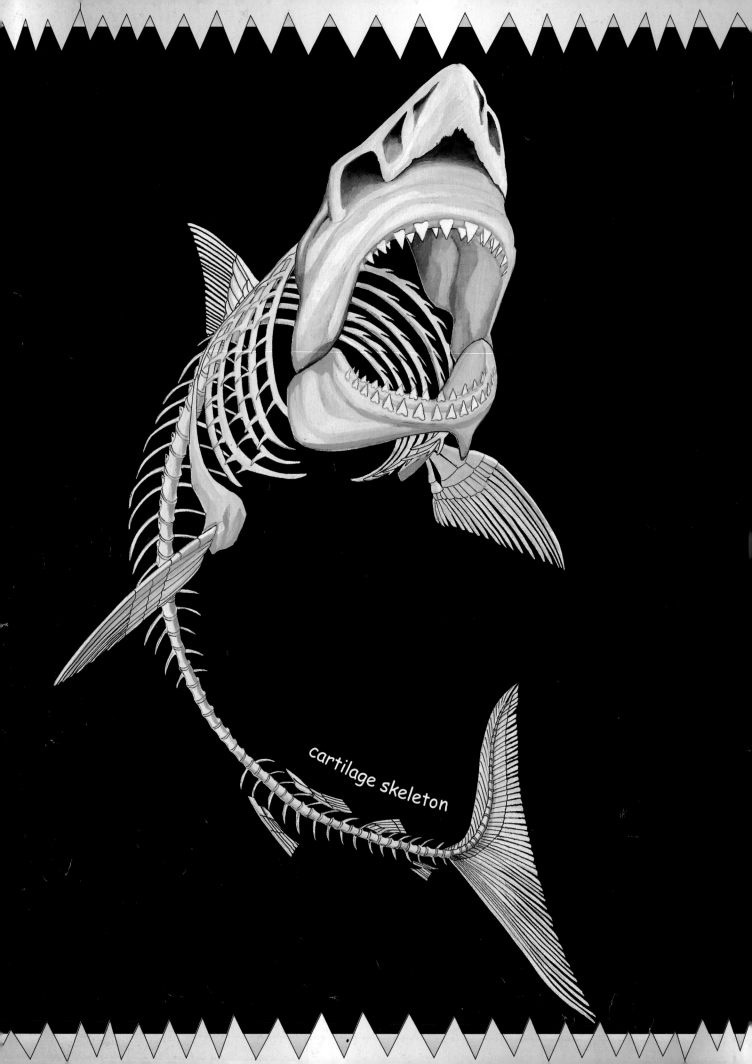

cartilage skeleton

# What is inside a shark?

The shark's skeleton supports its body. It also protects the internal organs – the heart, stomach and so on. The shark's spine or backbone runs all along the body, from the cranium (skull), which protects the brain, to the tail.

Sharks' skins are covered in denticles. The word means 'small teeth', which is what the denticles look like up close.

Do sharks breathe with lungs?

No, sharks breathe with gills.

gills

Sharks have five, six or seven gills on each side of their throat. Water from the shark's mouth passes over the gills. The tiny blood vessels in the gills take in oxygen from the water.

# How do sharks swim?

Swimming in the sea is much harder than walking on land. Most of a shark's body is made up of muscles attached to its spine.
A shark's streamlined body means it can move quickly and easily through the water.

## Did you know?

Sharks' livers are full of oil. This gives them buoyancy (the ability to float) and means that they do not need to use too much energy when they swim.

**Basking shark near the surface of the sea**

Basking sharks swim with their mouths wide open to catch the tiny plankton they feed on.

Bony fish have swim bladders to control their depth in the sea. Sharks don't have swim bladders. This means that if a shark stopped swimming, it would sink and die.

Great white shark

The great white shark is a killer. It eats seals, penguins and other sharks. It has also attacked people who are swimming in the ocean. It can grow up to 6 m long and is very aggressive.

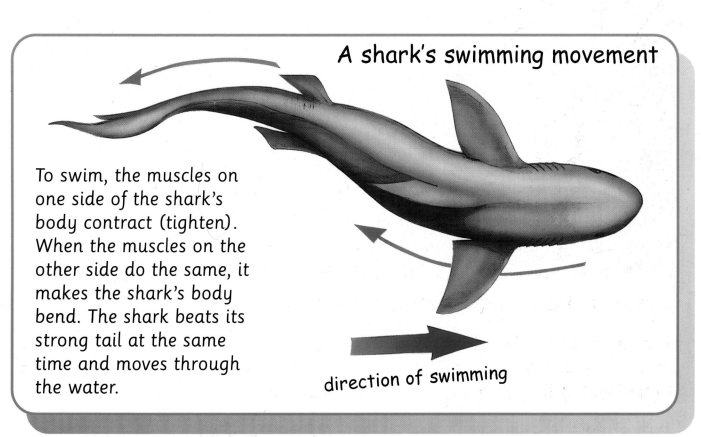

A shark's swimming movement

To swim, the muscles on one side of the shark's body contract (tighten). When the muscles on the other side do the same, it makes the shark's body bend. The shark beats its strong tail at the same time and moves through the water.

direction of swimming

# How do sharks hear and smell?

Sharks can hear, smell and see extremely well.
They don't have ear lobes like people do,
but a shark's hearing is probably better.
The semicircular canals in a shark's ears
help it to balance as it swims.

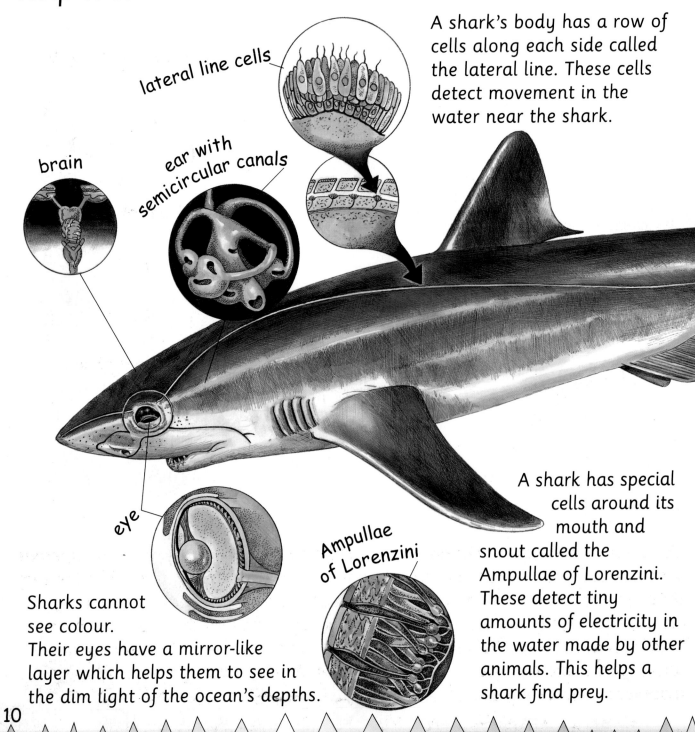

lateral line cells

A shark's body has a row of cells along each side called the lateral line. These cells detect movement in the water near the shark.

brain

ear with semicircular canals

eye

Sharks cannot see colour.
Their eyes have a mirror-like layer which helps them to see in the dim light of the ocean's depths.

Ampullae of Lorenzini

A shark has special cells around its mouth and snout called the Ampullae of Lorenzini. These detect tiny amounts of electricity in the water made by other animals. This helps a shark find prey.

## Did you know?

A hammerhead shark's nostrils are at each end of the 'hammer' of its head. When it smells blood in both nostrils, the shark knows the prey is straight ahead, even if it is half a kilometre away.

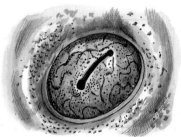

eye of an epaulette shark

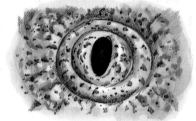

eye of an angel shark

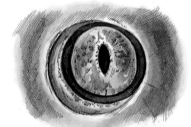

eye of a reef shark

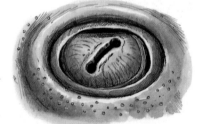

eye of a horn shark

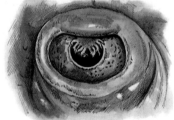

eye of a ray

scales covering pit organs

On the underside of sharks are sensitive cells that scientists call pit organs, protected by special scales. The organs are part of the shark's well developed senses although no one has yet discovered what they do.

Different sharks' eyes show the different ways they live. Fast hunters like the reef shark must be streamlined and they have eyes set into the head. Rays and sharks that live near the seabed, like horn sharks, hunt by sneaking up on their prey. Their eyes stand out more.

# Do sharks lay eggs?

All baby sharks are born from eggs, but not all sharks lay eggs! In many species of shark the eggs develop inside the female and she gives birth to fully formed young sharks called pups. Spurdog sharks develop inside their mother's body for between 18 and 22 months.

Port Jackson shark's egg

Yes, some sharks do lay eggs.

pelvic fin

Mating sharks swimming side by side

The female Port Jackson shark lays eggs protected in screw-shaped cases (above). She screws them into gaps in a rock for extra protection. Then, like all sharks, she swims away leaving the eggs to hatch on their own.

When sharks mate, the male holds the female with his pelvic fins and places sperm in the opening of her egg tubes.

## X-Ray Vision

Hold the page opposite up to the light and see what's inside a shark.

See what's inside

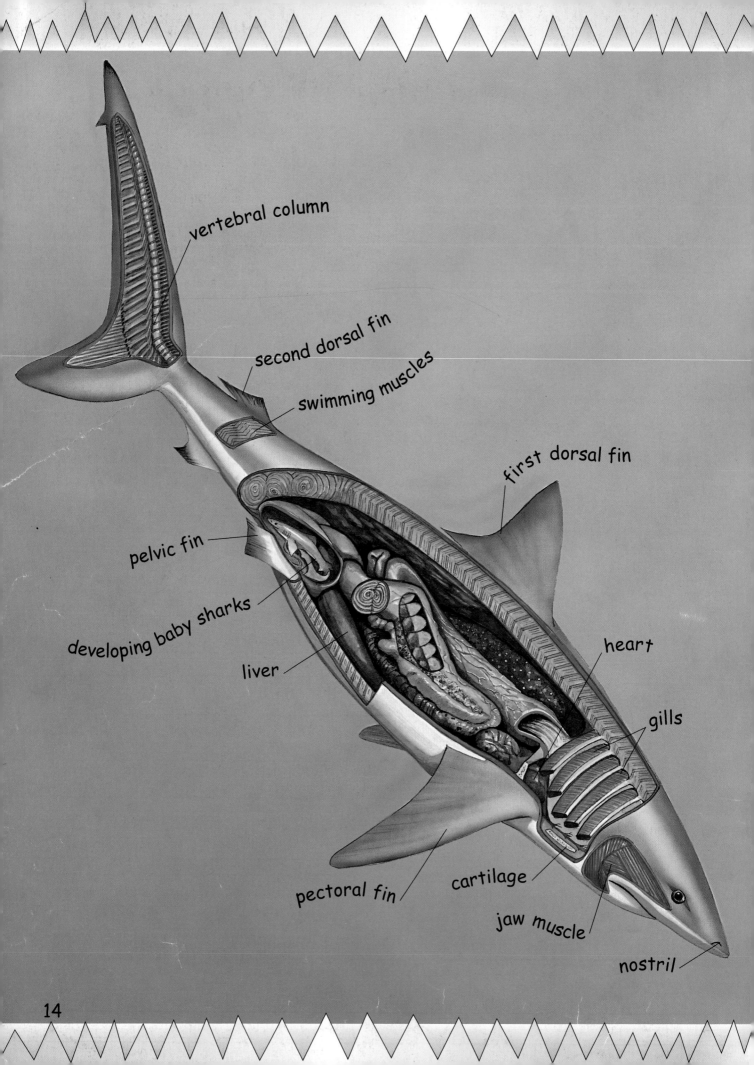

vertebral column

second dorsal fin

swimming muscles

first dorsal fin

pelvic fin

developing baby sharks

liver

heart

gills

pectoral fin

cartilage

jaw muscle

nostril

# How do baby sharks grow?

Inside each shark's egg is an embryo and a large yolk.

The embryo will develop into a baby shark, or pup.
The yolk is attached to the embryo and provides all the food the pup needs to grow. When the yolk is finished it is time for the pup to be born.

Newborn pups look just like small versions of adult sharks. Their parents do not look after them, so they must hunt for food straight away.

embryo    yolk

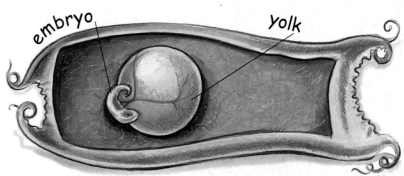

One-month old shark embryo

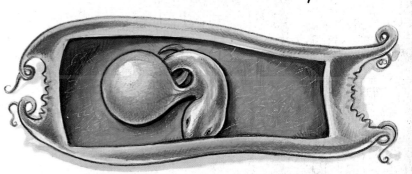

Three-month old shark embryo

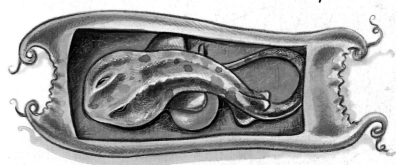

Seven-month old shark embryo

The best and safest place for any baby animal to develop is inside its mother. Developing embryos only protected by egg cases or shells might be eaten or smashed against rocks by rough seas. Sharks' eggs have tough, flexible cases. They often have long curly threads that become tangled in seaweed to stop them being swept away.

# What do sharks eat?

All sharks are carnivores, which means they eat other living creatures. But what they eat depends on where they live.

Mako sharks live in the Atlantic, Pacific and Indian oceans. There they catch squid and fish such as tuna and mackerel. Port Jackson sharks feed on sea urchins, shrimps and shellfish on the seabed around Australia.

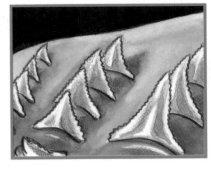

Sharks' teeth grow in rows that slowly move outwards towards the edge of the mouth. Teeth in the outer row become worn and fall out or get pulled out when biting. They are replaced by teeth in the row behind.

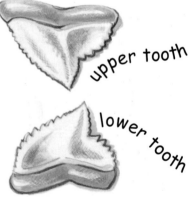

upper tooth

lower tooth

Sand tiger shark

The sand tiger shark has vicious-looking teeth used for catching fish in the shallow waters of the North Atlantic. The long, sharp inward-curving teeth help it to grip its slippery prey.

## Different types of shark teeth

lemon shark    tiger shark    sand shark

mako shark    dusky shark    bull shark

Sharks that eat different types of prey need different types of teeth. Long curved teeth grip prey. Blunt teeth crunch shellfish. Jagged teeth cut through flesh.

Basking sharks and whale sharks have tiny teeth because they just gulp seawater and feed on the plankton filtered out of it.

## Did you know?

The thresher shark has a long top part to its tail. When it finds a shoal of fish it thrashes the water with its tail. This forces the fish into a tight group and makes them very easy to catch.

Caribbean reef shark
catching fish

18 Whale shark with a diver swimming alongside

# Which shark is the biggest?

The two largest sharks in the world are the basking shark and the whale shark. Basking sharks grow to about 10 m. Whale sharks usually grow to 15 m, but some reach 18 m. Instead of being fierce hunters like most sharks, these huge creatures eat plankton and tiny fish.

**Basking shark swallowing seawater**

A basking shark gulps down about 9,000 litres of sea water an hour. As water passes through the gill slits, the plankton are filtered out.

## How big are whale sharks?

The scuba diver beside this whale shark (opposite page) shows just how huge these sharks are. Although the whale shark can swim fast if it senses danger, it normally moves quite slowly.

Whale sharks can weigh up to 13.2 tonnes!

**Plankton seen under a microscope**

Near the sea's surface it is warm and light. The millions of microscopic plants and animals that live there make up plankton.

Even when fully grown, dwarf sharks are only 15 cm long.

Dwarf shark     Actual size

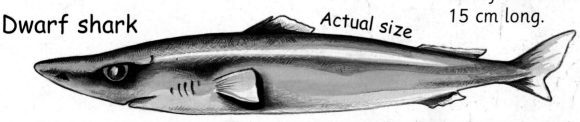

15 cm

# How do sharks hide?

Like all predators, sharks need camouflage. Tiger sharks have striped skins and leopard sharks have spotted ones so that they almost blend in with their surroundings. These sharks are difficult to see as they hunt among reefs or on the seabed.

Blue shark

From underneath, the pale belly of the blue shark makes it difficult to see against the light. The lesser sand shark's spots match the seabed (below).

Lesser sand shark

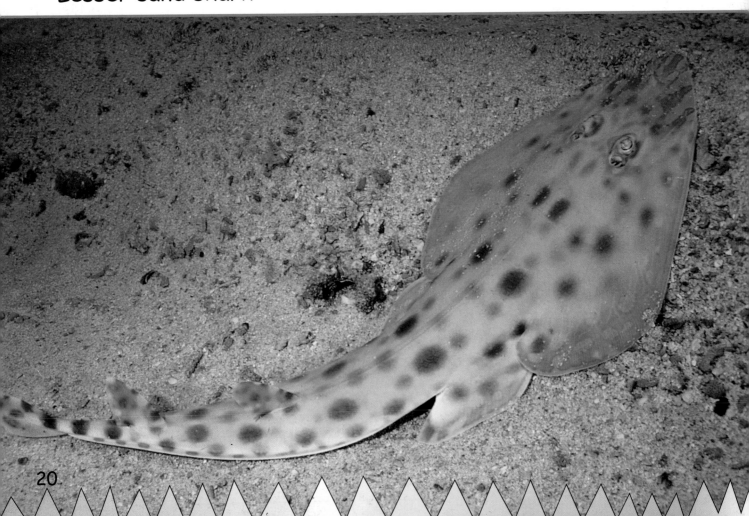

The wobbegong or carpet shark has skin coloured to look like the seabed and grows tassels that look like seaweed. Well camouflaged, it lies still waiting to grab a crab or passing fish.

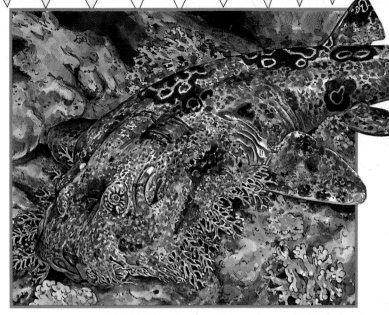

Wobbegong shark on the seabed

 Did you know?

The tiger shark is as fierce a hunter in the sea as the tiger is on land. The broken stripes on its skin make it very difficult for its prey to see. It hunts among the reefs of tropical seas.

Tiger shark

Angel shark

How do angel sharks hide?

Angel sharks live in the Mediterranean Sea, the Pacific Ocean and off the coasts of North America. Their skin is sand-coloured to look like the sandy seabed. They eat shellfish and fish such as dabs and soles. Angel sharks get their name from the two fins on their backs.

Angel sharks blend into the sand on the seabed.

**Great white shark**

The film *Jaws* shows sharks as fierce, aggressive animals that attack humans. The film is entertaining but it makes sharks seem scarier than they really are. Most sharks will never come close to people and will not harm anyone.

## Why are people scared of sharks?

Most people will never come across a shark in the wild. Sharks such as the great white have attacked people swimming off the coasts of Australia and South Africa but this does not happen very often. It is very rare for anyone to be killed by a shark.

stick with explosive

A punch on the nose will frighten away sharks that come too close. Divers likely to meet the great white shark, nicknamed 'white death', often carry a stick with them. It has an explosive on one end in case they are attacked.

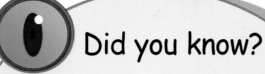

## Did you know?

Blood attracts sharks more quickly than anything else. They can smell it from several hundred metres away and every shark in the area will swim as fast as possible towards the smell. When they get to the blood they often become so excited that they attack each other.

Many species of shark live far out in the depths of the oceans so we know very little about them. That is another reason why myths about their fierceness have grown up. Some sharks will come and take bait (below), giving scientists a chance to study their jaws.

Great white shark taking bait

# Where do sharks live?

Sharks are cold-blooded which means they cannot control their body temperature. Sharks rely on the temperature of the water around them to keep their bodies at the right temperature.

## Did you know?

The mako shark is one of the world's fastest and strongest sharks. Makos catch swordfish which also swim extremely fast and can weigh 50 kg. The mako's dorsal fin often sticks up above the water as it swims.

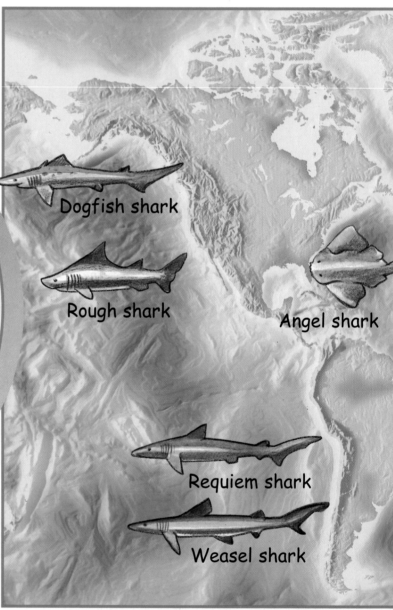

Dogfish shark

Rough shark

Angel shark

Requiem shark

Weasel shark

dorsal fin

Mako shark

When sharks live in groups, each member of the group is about the same size. If the sizes were mixed, the large sharks would eat the smaller ones.

Sharks cannot live in the Arctic or Antarctic Oceans because those areas are too cold for them. However, they can be found in all of the other oceans around the world. Many of the sharks pictured on the map (below) are found in more than one region of the world's seas. Very few sharks can live in fresh water.

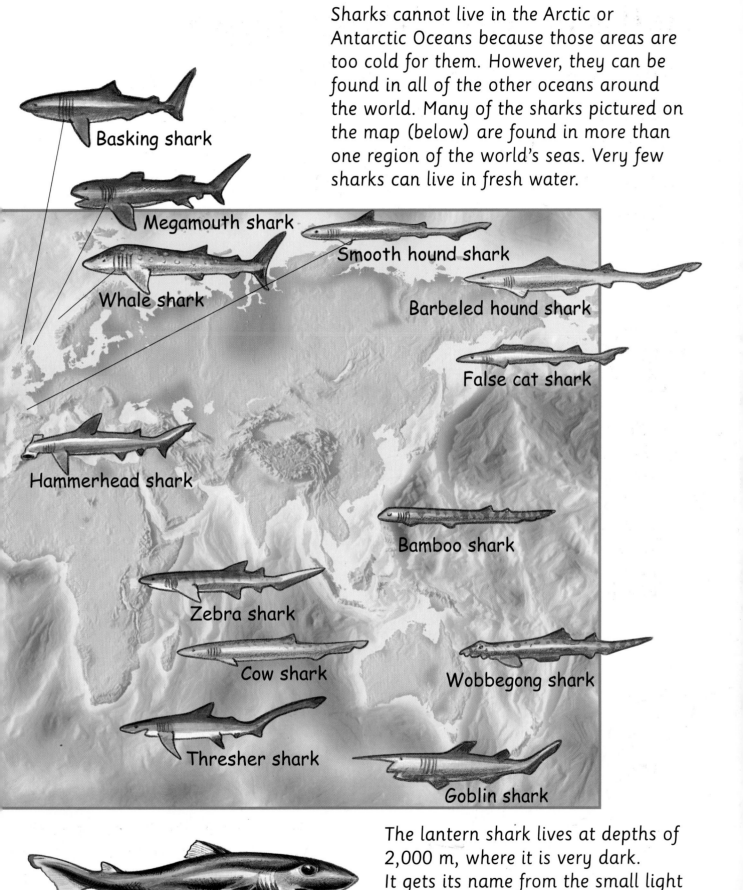

Basking shark

Megamouth shark

Smooth hound shark

Whale shark

Barbeled hound shark

False cat shark

Hammerhead shark

Bamboo shark

Zebra shark

Cow shark

Wobbegong shark

Thresher shark

Goblin shark

Lantern shark

The lantern shark lives at depths of 2,000 m, where it is very dark. It gets its name from the small light organs on its belly although no one knows how it uses them.

# Why are sharks killed?

Sharks are killed for many reasons. They are caught for their flesh, which is eaten or made into fertiliser. The oil from their livers is used in medicines and make-up.

Sharks are also killed for sport. Some species of shark have been hunted so much they are now in danger of becoming extinct.

Jaws and teeth of a sandbar shark

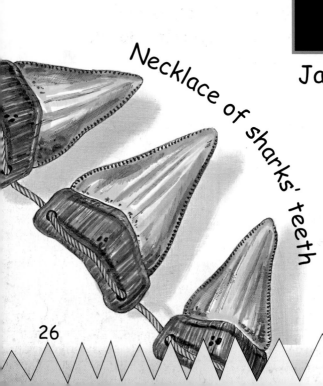

Necklace of sharks' teeth

Some tourist souvenirs are made of sharks' teeth, like this necklace (left). If people stop buying them, then perhaps fewer sharks would be killed to supply the trade.

Hunting and killing something for pleasure seems pointless when all that you have left of a magnificent living animal is its jaws to hang on your wall (above).

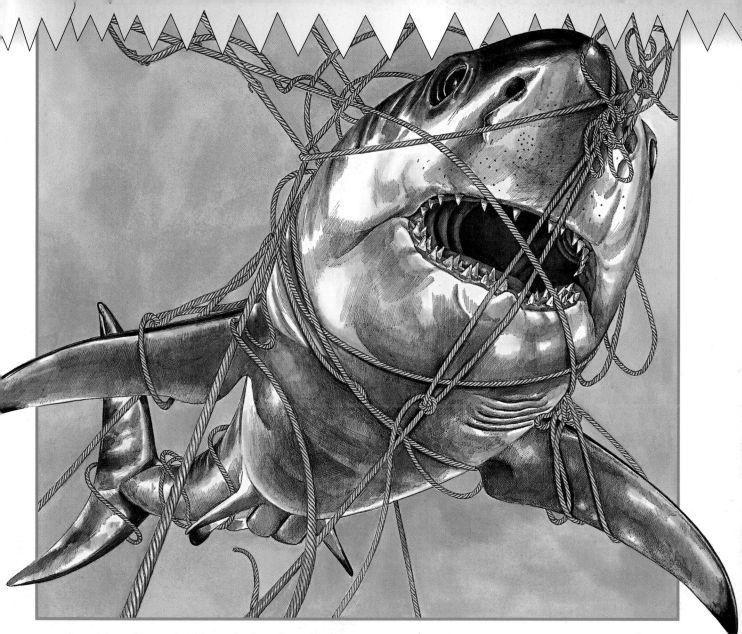

Each year thousands of sharks die tangled up in fishing nets and caught in the defence nets around swimming beaches. Most of these sharks would never have gone near a human, let alone attacked someone.

Sharks are sometimes killed for their skin. It can be made into fine bags and wallets and people pay high prices for it.

 Did you know?

The skin of sharks is so rough that in the past it was used to smooth and polish things. It was called shagreen.

Close up of the skin of a nurse shark

# Where can you see sharks?

A seaquarium, an aquarium for saltwater creatures, is probably the best place to see sharks. But keeping sharks in captivity is difficult. It is much better to see them in the wild. Some scuba diving holidays include the chance to swim with sharks.

### Did you know?

In 1960, a bathyscaphe, an underwater exploration vessel, dived to the deepest part of the ocean 11,000 m down. Some types of shark live that far underwater.

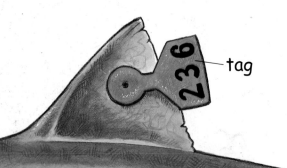

A Jacques Cousteau diving saucer

Jacques Cousteau, the French undersea explorer, helped design this 'diving saucer' (right) in 1959. Made of steel 2 cm thick, it let scientists observe sea life deeper underwater than ever before.

tag

Scientists catch sharks with bait. Each shark is then tagged with a number and a radio transmitter so it can be tracked once it has been let back into the sea. This helps scientists to learn about the movements of the different species of shark.

# Great white shark attacking a diver's cage

This great white shark (above) is attacking the shark-proof cage protecting the divers. It is important for scientists to be able to get this close to sharks and be safe. This is the best way to learn as much as possible about all sharks, but many are easily scared and studying them is difficult.

A seaquarium (below) is certainly the safest place to see sharks. You will be able to get really close-up views. But sharks need so much space that it is difficult to keep them happy and healthy in captivity.

## Viewing sharks in a seaquarium

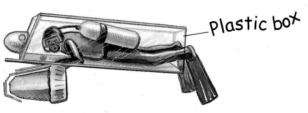

Plastic box

This diver (above) is protected by a special, tough plastic box and is quite safe as he swims up to sharks to study them.

# Shark facts

Female sharks have thicker skin than male sharks. This is to protect them from the males if they become aggressive during the breeding season.

The female mako shark usually gives birth to only one pup at a time. This is because the one pup has eaten any others that were growing inside its mother!

Young basking sharks are about 1.5 m long when they hatch.

The huge whale shark feeds upright. It rises to the surface, then sinks tail first, gulping in water and the plankton it contains, as it goes down.

In 1976 sailors on an American ship found something caught on the anchor. It was an entirely new species of shark. It was named the megamouth and was 4.5 m long.

The cookie cutter shark's teeth are so strong that it can bite holes in the rubber used to coat submarines.

More than 300 species of shark live in the seas and oceans around the world.

The fossilised teeth of a mako shark have been found. They are still as sharp as when it had its last meal 75 million years ago!

Port Jackson sharks are also called pig sharks. They have large, downward-pointing nostrils that look like a pig's nose. The shark uses them to sniff out its prey on the seabed.

Fossils that have been found show that sharks were swimming in the Earth's seas and oceans 450 million years ago. Cladoselache, the oldest known shark, was 2 m long.

Because sharks do not have skeletons of bone the only shark fossils are their teeth. The rest of the cartilage skeleton rots away. One ancient shark, Carcharodon megalodon, had teeth about 11 cm wide and 15 cm long. The great white shark has teeth 3 cm wide and less than 4 cm long!

Carcharodon megalodon probably weighed about 20 tonnes. It became extinct only 11,000 years ago.

Rock salmon is another name for the dogfish, a small shark. Rock salmon and chips is eaten in Britain.

# Glossary

**aggressive** Something which shows fierceness.

**bathyscaphe** A vessel for exploring deep underwater.

**camouflage** A colouring or shape which helps an animal blend in with its surroundings.

**cartilage** The flexible, gristle-like material that sharks' skeletons are made of.

**cold-blooded** An animal whose body temperature changes according to the temperature of its surroundings.

**cranium** The part of the skull that protects the brain.

**denticles** The small tooth-like growths that cover a shark's body.

**embryo** A young developing creature before it is born.

**extinct** Species of animals that are no longer alive anywhere in the world.

**fertilise** To join male sperm and female eggs to produce young.

**fossil** The very old remains of a plant or animal.

**gills** The organs that sharks and fish use to breathe.

**microscopic** Something so tiny it can only be seen under a microscope, not with the naked eye.

**plankton** The microscopic plants and animals that live near the surface of the sea.

**predator** An animal that hunts other living creatures for food.

**prey** Animals that are hunted by other animals for food.

**shoal** A large group of fish.

**species** A group of living things that share at least one feature and can breed together.

**streamlined** Something that is able to move easily through air or water.

**swim bladder** An air-filled sac that bony fish use to control their depth when swimming.

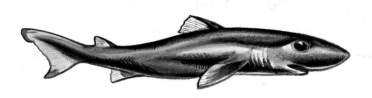

# Index